Happy Reading

Ella really loved stars and planets.
Every night, she would look up at the sky and imagine what it would be like to go to space.

One day, while watching TV, Ella saw a video of an astronaut floating around in space.

Ella was fascinated by space exploration and knew she wanted to be a part of it someday.

When Ella turned 8 years old, her parents got her a brand new telescope! It was always by her side on starry nights.

Ella's favorite teacher, Mrs. Garcia, talked to her about space exploration.

She told Ella all about rockets and spaceships that could fly to other planets!

She was so excited to learn more and dream about exploring the universe.

$\frac{x}{a} + \frac{y}{b} = 1$
hyp
opp
θ
adj
$\sin(\theta) = \frac{opp}{hyp}$

As she got older, Ella went to university to study space engineering. She took classes in math, science and many other fun subjects.

Ella never gave up, even when her classes were tough. She worked extra hard, and sometimes fell asleep studying!

..zzZZ

After 4 years of hard work, Ella graduated university and got her degree as an Engineer!

Ella got her dream job as an Aerospace Engineer building rocket ships that travel to space.

Ella loved watching the rocket ships blast off!

The view was absolutely breathtaking.

Ella helped build rockets that went to other planets, like Mars.

Now, those rockets are exploring and finding new and exciting things in the endless wonder of space!

The Lesson of This Story

If you have a big dream, don't be afraid to chase it! Even if it seems hard, you can do it if you believe in yourself. Just like Ella, who worked hard to make her dream come true, you can do the same. So don't give up, keep trying your best, and believe in yourself.

"Shoot for the moon. Even if you miss, you'll land among the stars!" – N.V.P.

What's Your BIG Dream?

Write down your top 3 big dreams

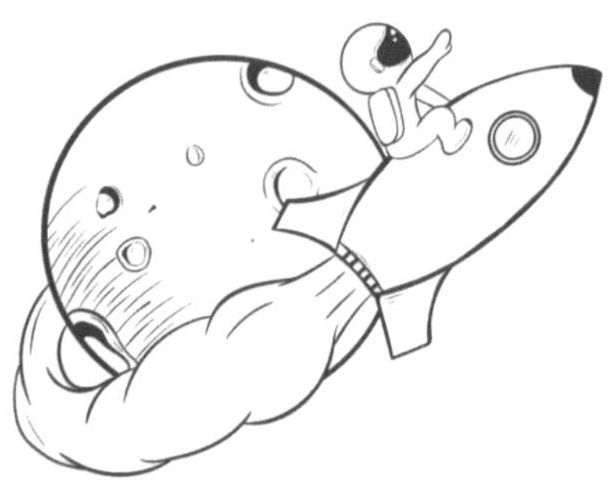

Find All The Hidden Astronauts In The Book!

Write down how many astronauts you found.

____

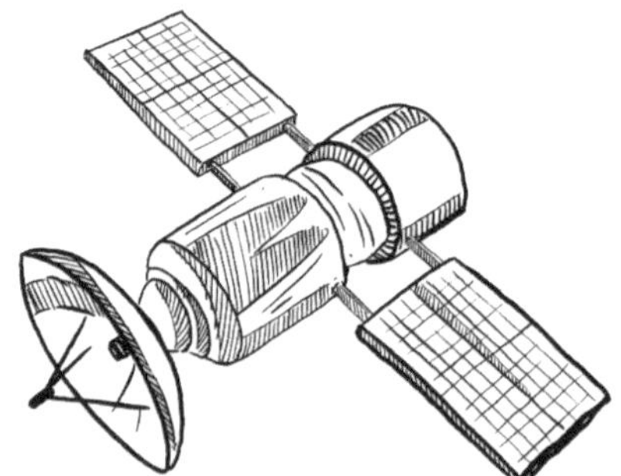

Help The Astronaut Get Back To Their Ship!

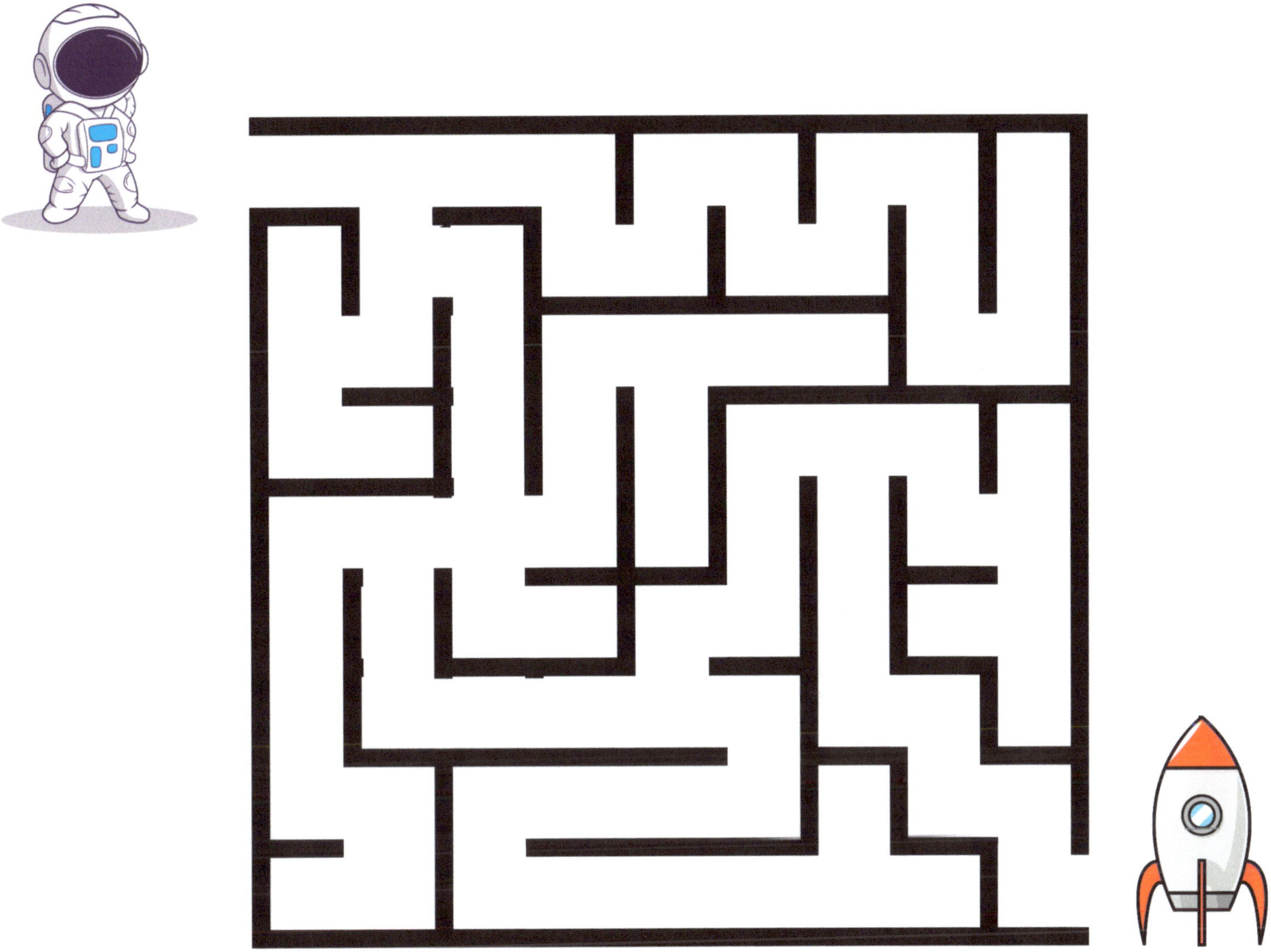

www.ingramcontent.com/pod-product-compliance
Lightning Source LLC
LaVergne TN
LVHW071111160826
845679LV00004B/1046
9781739030827